For a Godly Woman

_____

Presented By

_____

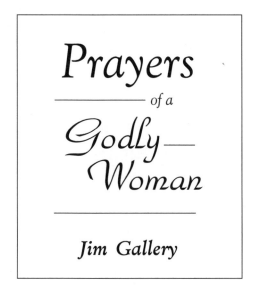

Prayers

of a

Godly Woman

Jim Gallery

BB

Brighton Books
Nashville, TN

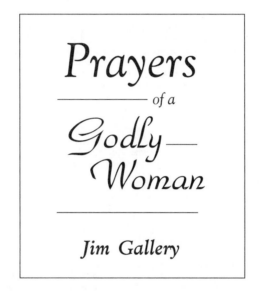

Prayers
—— *of a* ——
Godly ——
Woman

Jim Gallery

ISBN 1-58334-134-X

The quoted ideas expressed in this book (but not scripture verses) are not, in all cases, exact quotations, as some have been edited for clarity and brevity. In all cases, the author has attempted to maintain the speaker's original intent. In some cases, quoted material for this book was obtained from secondary sources, primarily print media. While every effort was made to ensure the accuracy of these sources, the accuracy cannot be guaranteed. For additions, deletions, corrections or clarifications in future editions of this text, please write BRIGHTON BOOKS.

All scripture quotations, unless otherwise indicated, are taken from the HOLY BIBLE, NEW INTERNATIONAL VERSION ©. NIV ©. Copyright © 1973, 1978, 1984, by International Bible Society. Used by permission of Zondervan Publishing House. All rights reserved.

Scripture taken from *THE MESSAGE*. Copyright © 1993, 1994,1995,1996. Used by permission of NavPress Publishing Group.

Scripture taken from the NEW AMERICAN STANDARD BIBLE®, Copyright © 1960, 1962, 1963, 1968, 1971, 1972, 1973, 1975, 1977, 1995 by The Lockman Foundation. Used by permission.

Scripture quotations marked (NLT) are taken from The Holy Bible, New Living Translation, Copyright © 1996. Used by permission of Tyndale House Publishers, Incorporated, Wheaton, Illinois 60189. All rights reserved.

Printed in the United States of America
Cover Design & Page Layout: *Bart Dawson*

1 2 3 4 5 6 7 8 9 10 • 01 02 03 04 05 06 07 08 09 10

Acknowledgments: The author is indebted to Criswell Freeman for his support and friendship and to the helpful staff at Walnut Grove Press.

In Dedication...

To My Mother,
A Prayer Warrior and a Godly Woman

Table of Contents

Help me, Lord:

Daily life is a tapestry woven together by the threads of habit. Our habits determine, in large part, who we are and who we become. If we develop habits that enrich our lives and the lives of others, we are blessed by God. If, on the other hand, we fall prey to negative thoughts or destructive behavior, we suffer.

No habit is more important to your life than the habit of daily devotion and prayer. God calls upon each of us to worship him with a thankful heart, and He instructs us to pray without ceasing. But amid the hustle and bustle of the daily grind, prayer and thanksgiving are too often neglected, even by those who know and love God.

This little book is intended as a tool for women as they develop and reinforce the habit of daily meditation and prayer. As such, the book is divided into 31 chapters, one for each day of the month. During the next 31 days, please try this experiment: read a chapter each day. If you're already committed to a daily worship time, this book will enrich that experience. If you are not, the simple act of giving God a few minutes each morning will change the tone and direction of your life.

May you find these pages a powerful reminder of God's grace, and may this daily exposure to God's wisdom be a blessing to you and your family.

13

Introduction

Godly women have had a profound influence on my life. As I remember schoolteachers, Sunday School teachers, friends, and family who invested in my life, I am humbled. God has richly blessed me with these women of faith.

I was humbled even more when I thought of the multitude of prayers offered up on my behalf over the years. No one has prayed more and harder for me than my mother. But there have been many others who have interceded on my behalf to a listening, responding God. From time to time, I hear that a godly woman — oftentimes a member of my church — is praying for me, and I am grateful. Other times, I am unaware of these prayers, but God knows, and that is more important.

This book is intended to encourage you to walk with God and to talk with Him. As you do, you will experience a growing sense of joy and fulfillment. As the old chorus states, "Every day with Jesus is sweeter than the day before." May all your days be lived in the caring arms of Christ, and may day each be a joyful testimony to His love.

Charm is deceptive,
and beauty is fleeting;
but a woman who fears the LORD
is to be praised.

Proverbs 31:30

Help Me, Lord To Love You More

"…Love the Lord your God with all your
heart and with all your soul and with all
your mind. This is the first and greatest
commandment."

Jesus
Matthew 22:37,38

Mary's actions stunned the dinner party. Instead of helping sister Martha serve the meal, Mary took expensive perfume and poured it on the feet of Jesus. Mary then wiped His feet with her hair. One disciple complained that the perfume could have been sold and the money given to the poor. He saw waste. Jesus saw love. "Leave her alone," Jesus said. "It was intended that she should save this perfume for the day of my burial. You will always have the poor with you, but you will not always have me." *(John 12:7,8)*

Jesus was preparing to endure a tremendous agony. The very same disciple who complained about Mary's extravagance would soon betray Jesus. Jesus would stand trial and be mocked, scourged, spit upon, and crowned with thorns. He would suffer the pain and humiliation of the cross. But, for a brief moment, Jesus experienced the devotion of a godly woman who was focused only on expressing her love for her Lord and Savior. Mary's was an extravagant love. Our love should be, too.

Love is not merely an attitude with which
God clothes Himself at certain times; rather,
it is an attribute that so permeates His being that
He could never divest Himself of it. To do so would
make Him less than God. Therefore, whatever
actions or commandments issue forth from His
throne must come from love.

Kay Arthur

Everything in your Christian life, everything
about knowing Him and experiencing Him,
everything about knowing His will, depends on the
quality of your love relationship to God.

Henry Blackaby

The grace of God is infinite and eternal.
As it had no beginning, so it can have no end,
and being an attribute of God,
it is as boundless as infinitude.

A. W. Tozer

Today's Prayer

*L*ord, I love You. Help me
to love You more. I can never give to
You more than You have given to me.
I can never love You more than You have
loved me. But today, I want to love You more
than yesterday. May my love for You be
evident in everything I do.

Amen

2

Help Me, Lord To Love Others

Some people are easier to love than others. When people are lovable, happy, and well-behaved, it is easy to like them and to love them. But, when people misbehave or do things that hurt us, love does not come easily. Still, Jesus says we must love even our enemies and pray for them. *(Matthew 5:44)*

Though it may seem impossible, we can love those who hurt us, but we need God's help. Elisabeth Elliot writes, "It is as we come to the Lord in our nothingness, our powerlessness, our helplessness that He then is able to enable us to love in a way which would be absolutely impossible."

We are commanded to love all our neighbors, not just the lovable ones. And when we fill our hearts with God's grace, He makes it possible to love those whom we could never love without the presence of a living God in our hearts.

If you are having difficulty loving or relating to
an individual, take him to God. Bother the Lord
with this person. Don't bother with him,
leave him at the throne.

Chuck Swindoll

Every experience God gives us, every person He
puts in our lives, is the perfect preparation for
the future that only he can see.

Corrie ten Boom

Dear friends, let us love one another,
for love comes from God.
Everyone who loves has been
born of God and knows God.
Whoever does not love does not know God,
because God is love.

1 John 4:7,8

Today's Prayer

*L*ord, I love You and want to obey
Your commands. You have asked me to
love my neighbors, all of them. I will try.
And when I fail, Lord, love them through me.
May all who see me know that I belong to You
because of my love for *all* people.

Amen

3

Help Me, Lord To Be Joyful

"Though you have not seen him,
you love him; and even though you do
not see him now, you believe in him and
are filled with an inexpressible and
glorious joy…

1 Peter 1:8

*T*o say that I looked forward to visiting Miss Amelia was something of an understatement. She was an elderly lady living in a small, frame home, and she brought revival and refreshment to my heart every time I was around her. Miss Amelia's eighty years on this earth had taken their toll on her physical body, but the years could never extinguish her joy for living. In fact, she seemed to love life more with each passing day.

*W*hen Miss Amelia's health began to fail, and as she spent her final days in the hospital, I observed a remarkable demonstration. She understood that death was near, yet she had no fear. She was utterly and completely prepared to be with her Lord, and she shared her dynamic faith with everyone she met. Even as her strength ebbed, she encouraged those around her. Doctors, nurses, nurse's aides and visitors all marveled at the joyous spirit of this godly woman. Miss Amelia was indeed "filled with an inexpressible and glorious joy." She loved God and God rewarded her. He will do the same for us, if we let Him.

It is not how much we have, but how much we enjoy,
that makes our happiness.

C. H. Spurgeon

Whence comes this idea that if what we
are doing is fun, it can't be God's will?
The God who made giraffes, a baby's fingernails,
a puppy's tail, a crooknecked squash, the bobwhite's
call, and a young girl's giggle, has a sense of humor.
Make no mistake about that.

Catherine Marshall

Some Christians are too full of the world to
enjoy God, and they are too full of God to enjoy the
world. They try to get the best of both. They get
neither or either.

Peter Marshall

Today's Prayer

*L*ord, remind me that the
joy I will experience today comes from You.
Remind me also, Lord, that the circumstances
I face this day and any day cannot rob me
of a sense of celebration and joy …
unless I allow it. Thank You for the
blessings You have given me. May I be
a joyous blessing to others, and
may I give all the praise to You.

Amen

Help Me, Lord To Know Your Peace

"Thou wilt keep him in perfect peace,
whose mind is stayed on thee…"

Isaiah 26:3 KJV

She was by my side everywhere I spoke, in church and in homes. Heija Kim was my translator on a mission trip to Korea. I would read from a Billy Graham tract entitled *"Peace with God,"* and she would interpret my words to the listeners. Heija and I spoke with hundreds of Koreans as we shared the message of God's peace.

We were told by missionaries that the tract had been chosen because of the universal need that all men and women feel for a sense of peace with God. Jesus has promised all believers a *"peace that passes all understanding."* (Philippians 4:7) Godly women, such as Heija, pray for and work for the peace that only comes from one source: the Prince of Peace, Christ Jesus.

God loves you and wants you to experience
peace and life—abundant and eternal.

Billy Graham

There may be no trumpet sound or loud applause
when we make a right decision, just a calm sense of
resolution and peace.

Gloria Gaither

I'm leaving you well and whole.
That's my parting gift to you. Peace....

Jesus
John 14:27

Today's Prayer

Lord, Thank You for the peace
I feel in my heart. Thank You
for calming me when I feel overwhelmed.
May the peace You provide for me
draw someone close, and
may I point them to You today.

Amen

5

Help Me, Lord To Have Patience

"I waited patiently for the LORD;
he turned to me and heard my cry.
He lifted me out of the slimy pit,
out of the mud and mire; he set my
feet on a rock and gave me a firm place
to stand. He put a new song in my
mouth, a hymn of praise to our God.
Many will see and fear and put their
trust in the LORD."

Psalm 40:1-3

The accidental death of her husband was devastating to the young mother. She was left with four small children to raise, and the insurance check would not last long. The first day of the rest of her life was long and lonely. She cried out to God for strength, but she felt so terribly weak and vulnerable.

Soon, however, she could voice thanks to God for the friends who had surrounded her with love and helping hands. Then, she found a satisfying job (with on-site childcare). Within a few years, she met a caring man....

God knows our circumstances and hears our cries. He leads us through the darkest days of our lives, and, in time, He puts a new song in our hearts. But God's timetable is His own. We must be patient. God is at work.

I do know that waiting on God requires the willingness to bear uncertainty, to carry within oneself the unanswered question, lifting the heart to God about it whenever it intrudes upon one's thoughts. It is easy to talk oneself into a decision that has no permanence, easier sometimes than to wait patiently.

Elisabeth Elliot

Patience is the companion of wisdom.

St. Augustine

To wait upon God is the perfection of activity.

Oswald Chambers

Wait for the LORD; be strong and take heart and wait for the LORD.

Psalm 27:14

Today's Prayer

*L*ord, I always seem to be in a hurry.
There seems to be so much to do and
so little time. Help me to live on Your timetable,
not my own. Give me patience, Lord,
and acceptance of Your will and Your way.

Amen

Help Me, Lord To Show Kindness

"...always try to be kind to each other
and to everyone else."

1 Thessalonians 5:15b

*W*hen Bonnie attended high school, she learned an important lesson about kindness from her mother, Mary James. Many poor families lived near the James' rural Georgia home, but one girl in particular impressed Bonnie. The girl was quiet and polite, yet extremely shy. And she wore the same tattered dress to school every day.

*B*onnie decided to give some of her clothes to the girl, and she asked for her mother's help. Mary James, in her wisdom, offered a suggestion: why not pick out clothes that the other students wouldn't recognize as Bonnie's? So Bonnie and her mother carefully selected an assortment of dresses and delivered them anonymously. Their act of kindness helped protect a needy child's self respect. And God smiled.

It is the duty of every Christian to be Christ
to his neighbor.

Martin Luther

I will be kind to the poor, for they are alone.
Kind to the rich, for they are afraid.
And kind to the unkind,
for such is how God has treated me.

Max Lucado

He who is kind to the poor lends to the LORD,
and he will reward him for what he has done.

Proverbs 19:17

Today's Prayer

Lord, You have poured out
Your kindness on me. I must do no less
for others. In my strong words and deeds,
and in my gentle words and deeds,
may I always mirror Your love and kindness
in my thoughts and my actions.

Amen

7

Help Me, Lord To Not Tire of Doing Good

"And God is able to make all grace
abound to you, so that in all things at all
times, having all that you need, you will
abound in every good work."

2 Corinthians 9:8

John Wesley said it well:

> Do all the good you can.
> By all the means you can.
> In all the ways you can.
> In all the places you can.
> At all the times you can.
> To all the people you can.
> As long as ever you can.

Grand expressions of generosity are wonderful, but I believe the small acts of goodness we do each day impact the world in a much greater way. One person at a time, one day at a time, one life at a time, we can bring kindness to those around us. And when we finish our day's work, God will say, "Well done, good and faithful servant!" *(Matthew 25:21)*

So let's not allow ourselves to get fatigued
doing good. At the right time we will harvest
a good crop if we don't give up, or quit.
Right now, therefore, every time we get the
chance, let us work for the benefit of all,
starting with the people closest to us in the
community of faith.

Galations 6:9,10

Let us not cease to do the utmost, that we may
incessantly go forward in the way of the Lord;
and let us not despair of the smallness of
our accomplishments.

John Calvin

Be ye therefore merciful, as your Father also
is merciful.

Luke 6:36 KJV

Today's Prayer

*L*ord, help me not only to dwell
on that which is good, but also to do
that which is good. Show me the countless
opportunities that come my way each day
to share Your goodness and loving-kindness.
May I never grow weary of doing good,
and may I always give You the glory.

Amen

8

Help Me, Lord To Be Secure in Your Faithfulness

"Because of the LORD's great love we are not consumed, for his compassions never fail. They are new every morning; great is your faithfulness."

Lamentations 3:22,23

I am thankful for absolutes. In a world afloat in a sea of relativism, we need anchors. One of those anchors is the constancy of God's faithfulness. He never changes.

Godly women understand that the Lord's immutable laws are not open for debate. Godly women seek God's will and they study God's Word. Godly women understand that people change, and circumstances change, but God does not.

There is great comfort in the knowledge that our Savior stands firm in a world filled with change. Paul writes to the Hebrews that Jesus Christ is the same yesterday, today, and tomorrow. *(Hebrews 13:8)* When the shifting sands of life throw us off balance, when friends disappoint us and circumstances confound us, God remains faithful, loving, unchanging, and, above all, present. Even before we reach out our hands to Him, He is there.

Not a star, not a planet, not a meteorite or
a quasar, no, not even a black hole is missing.
God made them. He knows their names,
knows exactly where they belong.
Can He not keep track of us?

Elisabeth Elliot

A mighty fortress is our God,
a bulwark never failing....

Martin Luther

Nothing happens by happenstance. I am not in
the hands of fate, nor am I the victim of
man's whims or the devil's ploys. There is One who
sits above man, above Satan, and above all heavenly
hosts as the ultimate authority of all the universe.
That One is my God and my Father!

Kay Arthur

Today's Prayer

*L*ord, I praise You for Your faithfulness to me.
I know that today and every day,
I can depend upon the constancy of Your love.
Help me to be faithful in my love for You as
You have been faithful to me. Hold me always in
the palm of Your hand, and keep me
ever-thankful for your unending grace
and for the gift of Your Son.

*A*men

Help Me, Lord To Pursue Gentleness

> "Cultivate inner beauty, the gentle,
> gracious kind that God delights in."
>
> *1 Peter 3:4 The Message*

This country was founded on rugged individualism. Most of us have been taught that ambition, perseverance, and hard work are important components of the American way, and, of course, they are. Successful women also understand the need of assertiveness and drive.

Yet, in a world that glorifies ambition, the Bible teaches that gentleness is a fruit of the spirit; thus, the godly woman will exhibit the virtue of gentleness in word and deed. On the surface, ambition and gentleness may seem to be mutually exclusive, but they aren't. Gentleness is strength under control.

The Bible gives examples of godly women who were successful in worldly endeavors. Deborah was a prophetess and judge used by God to deliver the children of Israel from oppression. *(Judges 4,5)* Lydia was a businesswoman chosen by Paul to begin a church in Philippi. *(Acts 16)* Esther courageously confronted her king to save her people. *(Esther 5:1)*

A gentle spirit is the hallmark of Christian maturity. Peter challenges the godly woman to cultivate gentleness because God delights in it. So should we.

You cannot cooperate with Jesus in becoming
what He wants you to become and simultaneously
be what the world desires to make you. If you would
say, "Take the world but give me Jesus," then you
must deny yourself and take up your cross.
The simple truth is that your "self" must be put to
death in order for you to get to the point where
for you to live is Christ. What will it be?
The world and you, or Jesus and you?
You do have a choice to make.

Kay Arthur

In everything, therefore, treat people the same way
you want them to treat you, for this is the
Law and the Prophets.

Matthew 7:12 NASB

Today's Prayer

*L*ord, please give me the strength to do
my best for You. May I give all of my
heart and soul to loving You and doing Your work.
And may those around me see gentleness
in my words and deeds as I live for
You today and every day.

Amen

Help Me, Lord
To Have
Self-Control

"God's readiness to give and forgive
is now public. Salvation's available for
everyone! We're being shown how to turn
our backs on a godless, indulgent life,
and how to take on a God-filled,
God-honoring life."

Titus 2:11, 12

The Bible teaches that we have choices. We can choose God's salvation in Jesus Christ, or not. We can choose to obey God's commandments, or not. We can choose to deny self and live for God, or not.

The godly woman chooses self-control. She resists (and avoids) the temptations of world as she seeks the joy and abundance that God has in store for her. She turns away from anger, jealously, and resentment. She chooses God's way not man's.

Jesus says that if we choose to follow Him, we will "learn to live freely and lightly."*(Matthew 11:30 The Message)* The godly woman understands that the decision to follow Jesus leads naturally to a life of disciplined freedom: the discipline to live according to God's laws and the freedom to live joyously in the love of Christ.

Faith is not a feeling; it is action.
It is a willed choice.

Elisabeth Elliot

Never be afraid to trust an unknown future to
a known God.

Corrie ten Boom

I am a spiritual being. After this body is dead,
my spirit will soar.
I refuse to let what will rot, rule the eternal.
I choose self-control.
I will be drunk only by joy.
I will be impassioned only by my faith.
I will be influenced only by God.
I will be taught only by Christ.
I choose self-control.

Max Lucado

Today's Prayer

Lord, You created me, and You are
molding me into an instrument of Your will.
Help me this day to abandon selfishness and
to avoid temptation. Let me seek Your plan
for my life as I choose to follow
Your word and Your will.

Amen

11

Help Me, Lord To Lift Praises to You

"Praise the LORD.
Praise the LORD, O my soul.
I will praise the LORD all my life;
I will sing praise to my God
as long as I live."

Psalm 146:1,2

After experiencing God's mighty deliverance from the Pharoah's army at the Red Sea, Moses and Miriam led the Israelites in a song:

> "The LORD is my strength and my song;
> he has become my salvation.
> He is my God, and I will praise him,
> My father's God, and I will exalt him."
>
> *Exodus 15:2*

We can understand the desire to praise God when good things happen. But what about praise when God's hand is not so evident? Fanny Crosby was a prolific hymn writer. She graced this earth for 95 years, and her songs are still found in most hymnals published today. Fanny Crosby was blind. Yet, out of this adversity, she found a depth of joy unknown to many. And she praised God in all of life's circumstances.

One of Crosby's most beloved hymns was "Praise Him! Praise Him!" The chorus reads:

> "Praise Him! Praise Him!
> Tell of His excellent greatness!
> Praise Him! Praise Him! Ever in joyful song!"

Fanny Crosby was a godly woman who praised God in good times and difficult times. Those of us who appreciate her music and worship her God should do no less.

In biblical worship you do not find the repetition
of a phrase; instead, you find the worshipers
rehearsing the character of God and His ways,
reminding Him of His faithfulness and
His wonderful promises.

Kay Arthur

Praise and thank God for who He is and for what
He has done for you.

Billy Graham

...let your light shine before men, that they may
see your good deeds and praise
Your Father in heaven.

Jesus
Matthew 5:16

Today's Prayer

Lord, I choose to praise You today.
Whatever circumstances may come my way,
I will praise You. You are my God,
You gave me life and salvation through
the sacrifice of Your Son. May all I do lead
others to glorify and praise Your name,
and as for me, Lord, I will praise
You today and forever.

Amen

12

Help Me, Lord
To Meditate On
Your Greatness

"I will sing to the LORD all my life;
I will sing praise to my God
as long as I live.
May my meditation be pleasing to him,
as I rejoice in the LORD."

Psalm 104:33,34

One can only imagine what went on in the heart and mind of Mary as she observed her newborn baby in the manger. The angels had already announced that she was God's choice to bear His son; then, she experienced the birth of Jesus in a stable. Soon, the shepherds paid their visit. These things must have seemed incredible and wonderful to a young mother. The Bible says, "…Mary treasured up all these things and pondered them in her heart." *(Matthew 2:19)*

In ancient times, God performed wonderful miracles. He still does. Miracles of love and kindness and goodness surround us every day; if we are still, and if we look for God's handiwork, we will see them. The righteous woman feels the hand of God's in her own life and in the circumstances about her. She, like Mary, meditates on these things and rejoices in the Lord.

As I quietly abide in You and let Your life flow into me, what freedom it is to know that the Father does not see my threadbare patience or insufficient trust, rather only Your patience, Lord, and Your confidence that the Father has everything in hand. In Your faith, I thank You right now for a more glorious answer to my prayer than I can imagine. Amen.

Catherine Marshall

The main thing that God asks for is our attention.

Jim Cymbala

Be still, and know that I am God...

Psalm 46:10

Today's Prayer

*L*ord, the busier I am, the more I need You.
Slow me down that I might see
Your wondrous works in my life and
in the lives of those who surround me.
As I discover anew Your glorious presence,
may my joy and thanksgiving be
a testimony to Your love, forever.

Amen

Help Me, Lord To Seek Your Will

"Father, if you are willing,
take this cup from me; yet not my will,
but yours be done."

Jesus
Luke 22:42

Sarah and Abraham had trouble trusting God, so they did it their way. God had promised them a son, but Sarah and Abraham believed Sarah was too old to conceive, so they devised an alternative plan. Abraham "helped" God by having a son, Ismael, by Sarah's maidservant, Hagar. *(Genesis 16)* But by straying from God's will, Abraham and Sarah created untold trouble for themselves and for future generations.

Elisabeth Elliot writes, "We are women, and my plea is let me be a woman, holy through and through, asking for the future that only he can see." The godly woman realizes that God knows what is best; she seeks to follow His will in all matters. God's plans are superior to our plans. Always have been. Always will be.

Every experience God gives us, every person
　　He puts in our lives, is the perfect preparation
　　　　for the future that only he can see.

Corrie ten Boom

There are two kinds of people: those who say
　　to God, "Thy will be done," and those to whom
　　God says, "All right, then, have it your way."

C. S. Lewis

If God, like a father, denies us what we want now,
　　it is in order to give us some far better thing
　　later on. The will of God, we can rest assured,
　　　　is invariably a better thing.

Elisabeth Elliot

Today's Prayer

*L*ord, help me know that Your will
for my life is always best. Your wisdom is
superior to my wisdom and You plan is superior
to my plan. When my desires are
different than Your desires, may
Your will be done. Always.

Amen

14

Help Me, Lord To Pray for Your Kingdom

"Ask the Lord of the harvest,
therefore, to send out workers
into his harvest field."

Matthew 9:38

I was traveling with associational missionary, T. B. Smith, inspecting the site of my youth group's summer mission trip. We were to visit a tiny hamlet in Michigan called Skidway Lake. The little town was home to a bank, a grocery store, a hardware store, an A & W Root Beer stand, and a single stop light.

T. B. introduced me to a very special lady, a godly woman who had prayed for many years that a church would be started in Skidway Lake. She had prayed diligently, consistently, earnestly, and still, no church. But the woman kept praying, and eventually, things began to happen.

T. B. Smith organized a Bible study; soon after that, a small group began to meet for Sunday services in a private home. Our youth group helped draw in more families, and finally: a church! The last time I inquired, several hundred people were attending services at Skidway Lake.

*T*he prayers of a godly woman did not go unheard. She prayed for a church, and God answered her prayers. He responded, as He always does, in His own time and with His own methods. Praise God, and praise godly women.

Go. This is the command of our Lord.
Where? To the world, for it is the world that
is on God's heart. Out there are multitudes
for whom Christ died. And the minute you and
I receive the light of the gospel we,
at that moment, become responsible
for spreading that light to those who are still in
darkness. Granted, we cannot all go physically,
but we can go on our knees.

Kay Arthur

Prayer is God's provision for us to know Him,
to know His purposes and His ways,
to experience His mighty presence working
in us and through us to accomplish
His perfect will.

Henry Blackaby

Watch ye therefore, and pray always....

Luke 21:36 KJV

73

Today's Prayer

*L*ord, Jesus commanded me to pray.
Let me pray not only for Your people
but also for Your kingdom here on earth.
Lord, help me to share Your gospel with
a world that desperately needs
Your healing grace. May I be
an instrument to share Your good news
today and every day of my life.

Amen

15

Help Me, Lord
To Have a
Servant Heart

"…whoever wants to become great
among you must be your servant…"
Matthew 20:26

She had me fooled. I grew up believing that Mom thought the best part of the chicken was the neck and back. No wonder. Whenever the plate of crispy fried chicken made the rounds at the dinner table, she always chose those two pieces.

Years later I understood—Mom had a servant's heart. She loved her family and did whatever she could to put their needs before her own, and she saved the toughest parts of the chicken for herself. Godly women are like that: they do for others before they do for themselves.

All too often, the world discounts the value of the servant's life. The message is faulty but clear: "Me first!" Jesus, however, showed us that serving others is the path to greatness in the Kingdom of God. God is impressed by those who are not impressed with themselves but are instead impressed with the needs of others. We should respond accordingly.

And so it was that a few nights ago, Mom cooked one of her famous fried chicken dinners, this time for a son with over 50 years life experience. And as I thought back on my mother's life, and her love, and her many years sacrifice, I picked up a fork and said, "Hey Mom, pass the chicken. And this time, may I please have the back?" It was the best chicken I ever tasted.

If we just give God the little that we have,
we soon discover he is all we really need.

Gloria Gaither

How do you spell love? When you reach
the point where the happiness, security,
and development of another person is as much a
driving force to you as your own happiness,
security, and development, then you have
a mature love. True love is spelled G-I-V-E.
It is not based on what you can get,
but rooted in what you can give
to the other person.

Josh McDowell

Your attitude should be the same as that
of Christ Jesus: Who, being in very nature God,
did not consider equality with God something
to be grasped, but made himself nothing,
taking the very nature of a servant…

Philippians 2:5-7

Today's Prayer

*L*ord, I want to be a servant.
Help me to be more concerned with
the welfare of others than with my own.
May I love my neighbors and demonstrate
that love through words and,
most importantly, through deeds.
And, Lord, when my actions reflect
Your love and Your grace,
may the world see You through me.

Amen

16

Help Me, Lord To Have a Joyous Attitude

"You were taught, with regard to
your former way of life, to put off
your old self…to be made new in
the attitude of your minds; and to
put on the new self, created to be
like God in true righteousness
and holiness."

Ephesians 4:22-24

Billy Graham is one of the most beloved men of our time. He is universally loved and respected. But it wasn't always so. Early in his ministry, he had many detractors who criticized his style and his methods of preaching. Ruth Graham knew that if she and her husband were to survive in the public spotlight, they would need to maintain the right attitude. Her advice was simple: "Just pray for a tough hide and a tender heart."

When we come to Christ, we are new creatures, and many old things must pass away. *(2 Corinthians 5:17)* Paul admonishes us to put on a new attitude. Christians with chronically negative attitudes miss the point: Of all people on this earth, we Christians have the most reason for optimism. After all, we belong to God, we enjoy His fellowship, and we receive His salvation. And besides, as Christians we know God's story, and we know what He ultimately has in store for us: a happy ending.

We cannot change our past. We cannot change
the fact that people act in a certain way.
We cannot change the inevitable.
The only thing we can do is play
the one string we have,
and that is our attitude.

Chuck Swindoll

Acceptance says, True, this is my situation at
the moment. I'll look unblinkingly at
the reality of it. But I'll also open my hands
to accept willingly whatever
a loving Father sends me.

Catherine Marshall

Today's Prayer

*L*ord, may my attitude be a reflection
of the great blessings of life You
have given to me. Help me always
to keep Your joy in my heart.
Help me to encourage everyone I meet,
and let me always give thanks to You
for Your love, for Your gifts,
and, above all, for Your Son.

Amen

17

Help Me, Lord To Express Hope

"We have this hope as an anchor for
the soul, firm and secure...."

Hebrews 6:19

In ancient days, low tides could prevent a ship from reaching the harbor. If the waters were too shallow, a sandbar might block the ship from entering port. To secure the ship while waiting for the tide to rise, a sailor would be dispatched in a small boat carrying the ship's anchor. The sailor would then carry the anchor across the sandbar and secure it. In calm or storm, the ship was safe because the anchor was firm.

Hope is a precious commodity in a difficult world. When trouble arrives at our doorstep, we are tempted to abandon hope. But God is there, too, knocking quietly, even in the darkness of our despair.

The godly woman knows the power of hope and she knows the power of God. She places her trust in God and puts her hope in Him. As the hymn writer Edward Mote writes, "On Christ the solid rock I stand; all other ground is sinking sand." Christ is the solid rock that gives us assurance and hope, today and every day. Without Him, we are adrift. With Him, we are secure.

Everything that is done in the world is done by hope.

Martin Luther

Why are you downcast, O my soul?
Why so disturbed within me?
Put your hope in God, for I will yet praise him,
my Savior and my God.

Psalm 42:5

There is never a time when we may not hope
in God. Whatever our necessities,
however great our difficulties, and though
to all appearance help is impossible,
yet our business is to hope in God, and it will be
found that it is not in vain.

George Mueller

Today's Prayer

*L*ord, it is so easy to feel despair
when I look at a world filled with so much
hopelessness. Remind me this day Lord
of the great gift I have to give to others:
hope. My hope is in Jesus Christ who
gives meaning and purpose to this life and
an eternal home in the next. May I share
His gifts this day and every day.

Amen

Help Me, Lord To Forgive

"Bear with each other and forgive
whatever grievances you may have
against one another. Forgive as
the Lord forgave you."

Colossians 3:13

Forgiveness is difficult. To forgive those who have hurt us (or hurt those we love) requires all the mercy we can conjure up. That's why I can't imagine what it took for Corrie ten Boom to forgive.

Corrie ten Boom experienced the horrors of a German concentration camp during WWII, yet, she somehow found it in her heart to forgive her captors. Despite the torture she endured, she forgave. Despite her pain and her losses, she forgave. Despite the normal human tendency to respond to hatred with more hatred, she forgave. And every time Corrie ten Boom forgave he captors, she, in turn, modeled godly forgiveness.

Jesus commands us to forgive those who have sinned against us. He warns us that we should forgive others so that we, too, might be forgiven. *(Matthew 6:12)* And when we do forgive, we learn a lesson that Corrie ten Boom learned long ago in the crucible of her suffering and pain: hate imprisons life, but forgiveness liberates it.

Forgiveness is not an emotion…
Forgiveness is an act of the will,
and the will can function regardless of the
temperature of the heart.

Corrie ten Boom

When the train goes through a tunnel and
the world gets dark, do you jump out?
Of course not. You sit still and trust
the engineer to get you through.

Corrie ten Boom

Only the truly forgiven are truly forgiving.

C. S. Lewis

Our Savior kneels down and gazes upon
the darkest acts of our lives. But rather than
recoil in horror, he reaches out in kindness
and says, "I can clean that if you want."
And from the basin of his grace, he scoops
a palm full of mercy and washes our sin.

Max Lucado

Today's Prayer

Lord, Thank You for the forgiveness
You have given me. May I, in turn,
be forgiving to others. Help me, Lord,
to cleanse my heart of bitterness and
regret so that You may then fill it
with Your grace and Your love.

Amen

Help Me, Lord To Be Strong in Adversity

> "I consider that our present sufferings
> are not worth comparing with the glory
> that will be revealed in us."
>
> *Roman 8:18*

All those who know of Joni Eareckson Tada are inspired by her story. As a teenager Joni was paralyzed when she dove into shallow water. She struggled over the next months trying to make sense of what had happened to her. Over time, her faith prevailed. Through her books and her testimonies, she has encouraged millions.

God's grace is sufficient for any difficulty we face. If we let Him, God can take our tragedy and turn it into triumph. As the psalmist writes, "Weeping may remain for a night, but rejoicing comes in the morning." *(Psalm 30:5)*

Faith in small things has repercussions that ripple
all the way out. In a huge, dark room,
a little match can light up the place.

Joni Eareckson Tada

The greatest sermons I have ever heard
were not preached from pulpits,
but from sickbeds.

M. R. DeHaan

When we are in a situation where Jesus
is all we have, we soon discover
He is all we really need.

Gigi Graham Tchividjian

Today's Prayer

*L*ord, forgive me when I complain
about my troubles. You have promised
I will not be tested beyond that which
I can stand. I believe Your promise.
Help me, Lord, to learn Your lessons in
good circumstances and bad, and help me
to share those lessons with a world that so
desperately needs Your love and salvation.

Amen

20

$\mathcal{H}\varepsilon lp$ $\mathcal{M}\varepsilon$, $\mathcal{L}ord$

$\mathcal{T}o$ $\mathcal{B}\varepsilon$ a

$\mathcal{W}orthy$ $\mathcal{T}\varepsilon acher$

"Pay close attention, friend, to what
your father tells you; never forget what
you learned at your mother's knee."
Proverbs 1:8 The Message

All of us are teachers. Some of us may be college professors, and some of us may teach Sunday School. Some of us teach at work while others teach at home. Perhaps we instruct in a formal setting, or perhaps we teach informally by the examples we set for others. Whatever our stations in life, and whatever our professions, we all are teachers because we all share lessons with others through our words and our actions.

Paul encourages Timothy to learn God's message and then to share that message with others. *(2 Timothy 2:2)* The godly woman understands that Paul's instructions apply not just to Timothy but to her.

As teachers, we must seek always to teach that which is holy and good. When we do, God smiles and the angels rejoice. But if ever we lead others astray, we invite sorrow into their lives as well as our own. So the lesson is simple: Live well, teach well, worship God, and follow His Son. Class dismissed.

The purpose of the Bible is to bring men to Christ,
to make them holy and prepare them for heaven.
In this it is unique among books,
and it always fulfills its purpose.

A. W. Tozer

Walking in faith brings you to the Word of God,
the Balm of Gilead. There you will be healed,
cleansed, fed, nurtured, equipped, matured
and hear God's "well done" because you have taken
Him at His Word.

Kay Arthur

When you believe that nothing significant
can happen through you, you have said
more about your belief in God than you
have said about yourself.

Henry Blackaby

Today's Prayer

*L*ord, Thank You for all those who
have invested in my life. You have
shown me many righteous teachers that
I might know Your Word and Your will
for my life. Use me, Lord, to help
teach others about Your love, Your grace,
and, above all, Your Son.

Amen

21

Help Me, Lord To Be an Example of Faith

"Now faith is being sure of what
we hope for and certain of
what we do not see."

Hebrews 11:1

The apostle Paul was impressed with young Timothy's sincere faith. Paul credited two godly women as the source of that faith: "I have been reminded of your sincere faith, which first lived in your grandmother Lois and in your mother Eunice and, I am persuaded, now lives in you also." *(1 Timothy 1:5)*

There were many men Paul could have chosen to mentor, but he saw something special in Timothy. That special quality was faith, a faith that began at home with the example provided by Timothy's mother and grandmother.

A woman of faith changes the world in at least two ways. First, she changes herself through the inner transformation that always accompanies a profound trust in our living God. Second, she transforms those around her by example and by outreach. What was true in the days of Paul and Timothy is equally true today: Women of faith change the world. Forever.

Sometimes when I was a child my mother or
father would say, "Shut your eyes and hold out
your hand." That was the promise of some lovely
surprise. I trusted them, so I shut my eyes instantly
and held out my hand. Whatever they were
going to give me I was ready to take.
So it should be in our trust of our
heavenly Father. Faith is the willingness
to receive whatever He wants to give,
or the willingness not to have what
He does not want to give.

Elisabeth Elliot

Faith is like radar which sees through the fog,
the reality of things at a distance that
the human eye cannot see.

Corrie ten Boom

Let us fix our eyes on Jesus, the author and
perfecter of our faith...

Hebrews 12:2

101

Today's Prayer

Lord, I believe, help my unbelief.
I trust, but help me trust more. Lord,
help me to focus on You and Your unwavering
faithfulness to me, so that I may, in turn,
be a living, loving example to others of the
transforming power of faith in You.

Amen

22

Help Me, Lord To Be a Witness

"…you will receive power when the
Holy Spirit comes on you; and you will be
my witnesses in Jerusalem, and
in all Judea and Samaria, and to
the ends of the earth."

Acts 1:8

*E*lisabeth married Jim Elliot. Several years later Jim was one of five missionary men killed by Indians in South America. Elisabeth Elliot went back to the same Indians who had killed her husband, and she shared her witness. Today, most of the Indians in that village are Christians, including some of those who helped kill Jim Elliot.

*E*lisabeth Elliot loved God and His people so much that she overcame fear and grief in order that she might minister to a people who desperately needed Christ's message. She had good news to share, and she was willing to go wherever God desired.

*M*ost of us are not called to be a witness in some remote area of the world. If we are, then we must be obedient like Elisabeth Elliot. But all of us are called upon to be witnesses to those around us. The Great Commission is our commission, today, tomorrow, and every day.

I lived with Indians who made pots out of clay,
which they used for cooking. Nobody was
interested in the pot. Everybody was interested
in what was inside. The same clay taken out
of the same river bed, always made in the
same design, nothing special about it.
Well, I'm a clay pot and let me not forget it.
But the excellency of the power is of God
and not of us.

Elisabeth Elliot

He would rather go to hell for you
than go to heaven without you.

Max Lucado

For the Son of Man came to seek and
to save what was lost.

Jesus
Luke 19:10

Today's Prayer

*L*ord, Thank You for loving me
so much that You saved me. You used others
to share that good news with me. May I be
used by You to proclaim that same wonderful
message to my friends and neighbors today
and every day.

*A*men

23

Help Me, Lord To Trust and Be Trustworthy

"…it its required that those who have
been given a trust must prove faithful."

1 Corinthians 4:2

Mary Magdalene stood outside of the tomb and wept. The body of her beloved Jesus was missing, and it was more than she could bear. Jesus had been unjustly tried, beaten, and cruelly put to death on a cross. Mary could not stand the thought that now someone had stolen the body.

A familiar voice silenced Mary's weeping. Jesus was speaking to her, "Go…to my brothers and tell them, 'I am returning to my Father and your Father, to my God and your God.'" *(John 20:17)* The very first person to see the risen Jesus was Mary Magdalene. The very first person entrusted with the good news of His resurrection was a godly woman, Mary Magdalene.

God has given us life through His Son, Jesus Christ. He has entrusted us with the privilege and responsibility to share that life with others. Now, we must share His message with a world in desperate need of salvation. And who better to share that good news than a godly woman…like you?

We must trust God. We must trust not only that
He does what is best, but that He knows
what is ahead.

Max Lucado

You will be able to trust Him only to the extent
you know Him!

Kay Arthur

...the Lord's unfailing trust surrounds the man
who trusts in him.

Psalm 32:10

Today's Prayer

*L*ord, You have trusted me with
the message of good news. You have
never failed me, help me never to fail You.
Every day, You will place countless opportunities
in my path to witness for Your Son Jesus.
Help me to share Christ's story
as I mirror His love.

Amen

24

Help Me, Lord To Be a Woman of Character

"All my fellow townsmen know that you are a woman of noble character."

Boaz to Ruth
Ruth 3:11

Everyone in town knew about Ruth. She had stood by her mother-in-law Naomi during Naomi's darkest hours. Ruth demonstrated loyalty to the one who had been loyal to her. Even when Naomi urged Ruth to leave and find a life for herself, Ruth replied, "Don't urge me to leave you or to turn back from you. Where you go I will go, and where you stay I will stay. Your people will be my people and your God my God." *(Ruth 1:16)*

Ruth was woman of integrity and strong character. This was her testimony to those who knew her. It is the same for godly women everywhere: their righteousness shines like a beacon for all to see.

The story of Ruth reminds us that character counts more than conversation, and that godliness counts more than good intentions. Then, as now, a woman is known by the character she keeps.

Persons of true godly character are neither
optimists nor pessimists, but realists who have
confidence in God.

Warren Wiersbe

The things that matter most in this world,
they can never be held in your hand.

Gloria Gaither

The best way to show up a crooked stick,
is to lay a straight one beside it.

Ruth Graham

Today's Prayer

*L*ord, Help me to be a person of integrity.
May my motive always be to please You
by doing what is right. And, if others
observe me to be a person of noble character,
I give you all honor and glory, for all that
I am and all that I have is Yours.

Amen

25

Help Me, Lord To Work Diligently

"She sets about her work vigorously…"
Proverbs 31:17

Jesus loved Martha and her family. The depth of that love was expressed when he wept at Lazarus' death. *(John 11:35)* Martha was a doer, a worker, a woman who always put the needs of others before her own. And Jesus loved her.

The writer of Proverbs identifies the godly woman as one who is industrious, working in the home (by taking care of the family's needs), and working outside the home (buying land and trading for needed goods). *(Proverbs 31:15-18)* The godly woman, whether she works at home, away from home, or both, knows the truth of the ancient couplet: "A man works from sun to sun, but a woman's work is never done." But it's worth it. Just ask Martha.

Whatever you do, work at it with all your heart,
as working for the Lord, not for men....

Colossians 3:23

You cannot stay where you are and go with God.
You cannot continue doing things your way and
accomplish God's purposes in His ways.
Your thinking cannot come close to God's thoughts.
For you to Do the will of God, you must adjust your
life to Him, His purposes, and His ways.

Henry Blackaby

God has plans—not problems—for our lives.
Before she died in the concentration camp in
Ravensbruck, my sister Betsie said to me,
"Corrie, your whole life has been a training for the
work you are doing here in prison—and for the work
you will do afterward."

Corrie ten Boom

Today's Prayer

*L*ord, You have created me for a purpose.
Help me to work vigorously and passionately
do fulfill that purpose. May I see
every opportunity for work as
an opportunity to serve
Your children and honor You.

*A*men

26

Help Me, Lord To Be Part of Your Plan

"Then his sister asked Pharoah's daughter, 'Shall I go and get one of the Hebrew women to nurse the baby for you?'"

Exodus 2:7

When Miriam saw the Pharoah's daughter discover her baby brother Moses, Miriam devised a plan. With the Pharoah's daughter's blessing, Miriam arranged for the very mother of Moses to be the baby's nursemaid. How ironic. The Pharoah, afraid that a leader of the Hebrews would arise, ordered all male children to be put to death. Yet the very one the Pharoah wanted to kill was raised by the Pharoah's own daughter, with the child's mother as nanny.

God's ways are not our ways. His plans don't always fit with the plans we make. Sometimes, His plans are incomprehensible to us, but godly women, like Miriam, remain faithful. They seek out God's plan and follow it whether they understand it fully or not.

Perhaps you are facing a difficult decision. Perhaps you are confused, or worried, or frightened. If so, remember that God remains in His heaven, watching over His children. And remember that God has a plan that includes you as an integral part. Your task is straightforward: keep praying and keep searching for God's will in your life. His plan may be different than yours, and that's quite alright because your plan is manmade, but God's is heaven-sent.

God has no problems only plans.

Corrie ten Boom

The itch to know and to have and
to be anything other than
what God intends me to know
to have and to be
must go.

Elisabeth Elliot

He can accomplish anything He purposes to do.
If He ever asks you to do something.
He Himself will enable you to do it.

Henry Blackaby

Today's Prayer

*L*ord, even if I must make major adjustments
in my life, I want to be in the center of Your will.
Whatever glorious work that You have
planned for me, I wish to fulfill. Lead me
and guide me so that I might be a part of
Your kingdom here in earth, and prepare me
for the glorious day when I will join
Your kingdom in heaven.

Amen

Help Me, Lord To Be Wise

"Those who are wise will shine like the brightness of the heavens, and those who lead many to righteousness, like the stars for ever and ever."

Daniel 12:3

Old Testament judges were political, military, and spiritual leaders. They were highly esteemed for their wisdom. And judges were usually men, but not always. Deborah was a judge who was recognized by the Israelites for her wisdom and spiritual leadership. *(Judges 4,5)*

A godly woman is a wise woman. Her intimate relationship with God helps her make wise choices. A godly woman's respect for God's commandments makes her an insightful leader. Solomon writes of the godly woman: "She speaks with wisdom, and faithful instruction is on her tongue." *(Proverbs 31:26)* May God continue to raise up righteous women, and when these wise women speak, may the rest of us listen…carefully.

No matter how efficient, smart, or independent
we happen to think ourselves to be, sooner or
later we run into a "brick wall" that our intelligence
or experience cannot handle for us. We fake it,
avoid it, or blunder through it. But a better solution
would be to find someone who has walked that way
before and has gained wisdom from experience.

Gloria Gaither

If any of you lacks wisdom, he should ask God,
who gives generously to all without finding fault,
and it will be given to him.

James 1:5

Today's Prayer

Lord, Your path is the right and
righteous path. Thank You for leading me
on that path, and help me to always seek
Your wisdom in every decision I must make.
And, may every word I speak and
every step I take reflect Your wisdom and
my faithfulness to You.

Amen

28

Help Me, Lord To Care for the Needy

"…blessed is he who is kind to the needy."

Proverbs 14:21

Dorcas was dearly loved by friends and family. She wasn't a famous preacher or singer or prophetess. She was simply a good woman who was loved because of her acts of goodness and her care of the needy. *(Acts 9:36)* Dorcas cared for others in down-to-earth practical ways. We should do likewise.

Caring for the needy not only pleases God but also helps us keep perspective. We view our own problems in a more realistic light when we focus our energies on meeting the needs of others.

The godly woman balances her daily life with a lifelong ministry to those who are less fortunate than she. In doing so, she uplifts her community and, more importantly, she follows the will of the ultimate caregiver: God.

It's no secret. The ministry of the church is
a genuine concern for others. We need to stop
talking about it and start doing it. Rise and shine,
friend. Everyone you meet today is on
Heaven's Most Wanted list.

Chuck Swindoll

I was hungry and you fed me,
I was thirsty and you gave me a drink,
I was homeless and you gave me a room,
I was shivering and you gave me clothes,
I was sick and you stopped to visit,
I was in prison and you came to me.
"...Master, what are you talking about? When did we
ever see you hungry and feed you, thirsty and give
you a drink? And when did we ever see you sick or in
prison and come to you?" Then the King will say, "I'm
telling you the solemn truth: Whenever you did one
of these things to someone overlooked or ignored,
that was me—you did it to me."

Jesus
Matthew 25:35-40 The Message

Today's Prayer

*L*ord, open my eyes to Your Will.
Help me to see the world with Your eyes
so that I might not be blinded to the needs
of those around me. Use me to meet
the needs of Your children this day
and every day of my life.

Amen

29

Help Me, Lord To Be Bold in the Things That Matter

"For God did not give us a spirit of
timidity, but a spirit of power, of love
and of self-discipline."

2 Timothy 1:7

Something had to be done. Haman, confidant to King Xerxes, hatched a plot to kill the Jews. It appeared that only Esther, a Jew herself, might be able to save the Hebrew people. She was queen to King Xerxes but in no way his equal. To even walk into the king's presence without being summoned was to invite his wrath and, sometimes, to invite death.

But, this was Esther's moment. She boldly confronted the king with the plot of Haman and God was with her. King Xerxes received Esther, believed her, dispatched Haman, and the Jews were saved.

Esther was a godly woman who understood God's way was sometimes difficult, but she also understood that God would never desert her. Esther found that God would provide the boldness needed to accomplish His will and His way. And He still does.

What kind of a God is it who asks everything of us?
The same God who "...did not spare his own Son,
but gave him up for us all; and with this gift
how can he fail to lavish upon us all he has to give?"
He gives all.
He asks all.

Elisabeth Elliot

Really, then, our problem is not weakness,
but independence! And, in covenant,
you die to independent living.

Kay Arthur

Never be afraid to trust an unknown future
to a known God.

Corrie ten Boom

Today's Prayer

Lord, You always provide the plan.
Let me provide the boldness.
When I am fearful, Lord, give me courage
that I may always be ready to stand
for what is right and pleases You.

Amen

30

Help Me, Lord To Know Your Priorities

"But seek first his kingdom and his righteousness, and all these things will be given to you as well."

Matthew 6:33

She was a successful businesswoman, wealthy, and the head of her household. She led prayer meetings, and she held church in her home. She is not the busy, modern, 21st century woman. She is Lydia of the 1st century, the woman who impressed Paul as the one to join him in starting the Philippian church.

Lydia's life would appear to be as hectic as the lives of most modern women. Yet, Lydia, in the same 24-hour days we have, accomplished all she needed. God used her to create a church that Paul loved. He would later write to the church, "I thank my God every time I remember you. In all my prayers for all of you, I always pray with joy because of your partnership in the gospel from the first day until now…." *(Philippians 1:4,5)*

All women are busy. Godly women stay busy in God's work and under His direction.

...because God is my sovereign Lord,
I was not worried. He manages perfectly,
day and night, year in and year out, the movements
of the stars, the wheeling of the planets, the
staggering coordination of events that goes on at the
molecular level in order to hold things together.
There is no doubt that he can manage the timing of
my days and weeks.

Elisabeth Elliot

You may not know what you are going to do;
you only know that God knows what
He is going to do.

Oswald Chambers

Today's Prayer

*L*ord, Thank you for satisfying work to do.
The urgent demands of this world
sometimes crowd out the important.
Help me to hear Your voice
directing my activities this day.

Amen

31

Help Me, Lord
To Be an Encourager

"Joseph, a Levite from Cyprus, who the
apostles called Barnabas (which means
Son of Encouragement), sold a field he
owned and brought the money and
put it at the apostles' feet."

Acts 4:36,37

Joseph was such an encourager that the disciples renamed him Barnabas, "Son Of Encouragement." I never met Barnabas, but I have met the "Daughter of Encouragement," Angela Freeman. Angela has her hands full being a mother and a wife, yet she always finds time to encourage others, including me. She writes supportive notes; she makes gifts; she phones with uplifting words; she bakes banana bread to die for. Angela has many talents, but none greater than her ability to encourage her family and friends. God uses women like Angela to build His Kingdom on earth.

Each of us, in our own way, can become a powerful source of encouragement to others. Certainly, we do not all share the same gifts nor do we all share the same talents and abilities. No matter. What we do share is the ability to speak a kind word to a friend, or hand a cookie to a child, or give a pat on the back to someone who needs it.

God takes the business of encouragement very seriously, and for good reason. He takes our encouraging words and transforms them into greater things than we mortals can imagine. God's great kingdom is built, in part, by the kind words and good deeds of godly men and women the world over. No kindness is too small to be a part of God's plan. Not even a slice of banana bread.

To believe in your dreams,
   To share your joys,
   To dry your tears.
   To give you hope,
  To comfort your hurts,
   To listen.
  To laugh with you,
 To show you a better way,
  To tell you the truth,
  To encourage you.
Who else can do that for you?
That's what friends are for.

Anonymous

Let's see how inventive we can be
 in encouraging love and helping out...

Hebrews 10:24

Today's Prayer

Lord, You have blessed me with
many friends and encouragers.
Thank You for that blessing. Help me
to be a constant blessing to others
as I look for ways to inspire and uplift
my friends and family.

Amen

Selected Bible Verses

God Calls Upon Us
to Show Kindness to Others

Be ye therefore merciful, as your Father
also is merciful.

Luke 6:36 KJV

A kind man benefits himself,
but a cruel man brings trouble on himself.

Proverbs 11:17 NIV

A gentle answer turns away wrath,
but a harsh word stirs up anger.

Proverbs 15:1 NIV

A new commandment I give unto you,
That ye love one another; as I have loved you....

John 13:34 KJV

...Verily I say unto you, Inasmuch as ye have done it
unto one of the least of these my brethren,
ye have done it unto me.

Matthew 25:40 KJV

In Times of Struggle, God Gives Us Comfort

The Lord is my shepherd; I shall not want.

Psalm 23:1 KJV

Every word of God is flawless; he is a shield
to those who take refuge in him.

Proverbs 30:5 NIV

Give us help from trouble:
for vain is the help of man.

Psalm 60:11 KJV

He giveth power to the faint; and to them
that have no might he increaseth strength.

Isaiah 40:29 KJV

For the eyes of the Lord are toward the righteous,
and his ears attend to their prayers.

I Peter 3:12 NASB

Trusting God

Trust the Lord your God with all your heart and
lean not on your own understanding; in all your
ways acknowledge him, and he will
make your paths straight.

Proverbs 3:5-6 NIV

The Lord says, "I will guide you along the best
pathway for your life. I will advise you and
watch over you."

Psalm 32:8 NLT

Submit yourselves therefore to God.
Resist the devil, and he will flee from you.
Draw nigh to God, and he will draw nigh to you.

James 4:7-8 KJV

The LORD is my rock, and my fortress,
and my deliverer; my God, my strength,
in whom I will trust....

Psalm 18:2 KJV

Commit everything you do to the Lord.
Trust him, and he will help you.

Psalm 37:5 NLT

God Calls Us to be
Humble of Spirit

Humble yourselves therefore under the mighty hand
of God, that he may exalt you in due time.

I Peter 5:6 KJV

…humility comes before honor.

Proverbs 15:33 NIV

And whosoever shall exalt himself shall be abased;
and he that shall humble himself shall be exalted.

Matthew 23:12 KJV

For I say, through the grace given unto me,
to every man that is among you, not to think of
himself more highly than he ought to think; but to
think soberly, according as God hath dealt to every
man the measure of faith.

Romans 12:3 KJV

Humble yourselves in the sight of the Lord,
and he shall lift you up.

James 4:10 KJV

The Power of Prayer

In my distress I called upon the Lord;
 I cried unto my God for help.
 From his temple, he heard my voice.

Psalm 18:6 NIV

I sought the Lord, and he heard me,
 and delivered me from all my fears.

Psalm 34:4 KJV

…for your Father knows what you need,
 before you ask Him.

Matthew 6:8 NASB

Ask and it shall be given to you; seek and
 you shall find; knock and it shall be opened to you.
 For every one who asks receives, and he who seeks
 finds, and to him who knocks it shall be opened.

Matthew 7:7 NASB

Cast your burden upon the Lord and He will sustain
 you: He will never allow the righteous to be shaken.

Psalm 55:22 NASB

When Questions Arise, Prayer is the Answer

In the day of my trouble I shall call upon Thee,
for Thou wilt answer me.

Psalm 86:7 NASB

And it will come about that whoever calls on
the name of the Lord will be delivered.

Joel 2:32 NASB

The Lord is far from the wicked but he hears
the prayer of the righteous.

Proverbs 15:29 NIV

…Our Father which art in heaven,
Hallowed be thy name. Thy kingdom come,
Thy will be done in earth, as it is in heaven.

Matthew 6:9-10 KJV

Watch ye therefore, and pray always….

Luke 21:36 KJV

A Thankful Heart is Pleasing to God ... and a Gift to Oneself

Make a joyful noise unto the Lord all ye lands.
Serve the lord with gladness: come before his
presence with singing. Know ye that the Lord he is
God: it is he that hath made us, and not we
ourselves; we are his people and the sheep of his
pasture. Enter into his gates with thanksgiving , and
into his courts with praise; be thankful unto him and
bless his name. For the Lord is good;
his mercy is everlasting; and his truth
endureth to all generations.

Psalm 100:1-5 KJV

Let the peace of Christ rule in your hearts,
since as members of one body you were
called to peace. And be thankful.

Colossians 3:15 NIV

In everything give thanks; for this is God's Will for
you in Christ Jesus.

I Thessalonians 5:18 NIV

God's Way Offers Us Peace

And as they thus spake, Jesus himself stood in
the midst of them, and saith unto them,
Peace be unto you.

Luke 24:36 KJV

Light shines on the godly, and joy on those
who do right. May all who are godly be happy
in the Lord and praise his holy name.

Psalm 97:11-12 NLT

And Jesus said unto them, I am the bread of life:
he that cometh to me shall never hunger; and he
that believeth on me shall never thirst.

John 6:35 KJV

These things I have spoken unto you, that in me ye
might have peace. In the world ye shall have
tribulation: but be of good cheer;
I have overcome the world.

John 16:33 KJV

On Serving Others

And he sat down, and called the twelve,
and saith unto them, If any man desire to be first,
the same shall be last of all, and servant of all.

Mark 9:35 KJV

Neither be ye called masters: for one is your Master,
even Christ. But he that is greatest among
you shall be your servant.

Matthew 23:10-11 KJV

Therefore, since we receive a kingdom which cannot
be shaken, let us show gratitude by which
we may offer to God an acceptable service
with reverence and awe.

Hebrews 12:28 NASB

Therefore all things whatsoever ye would that men
should do to you, do ye even so to them: for this is
the law and the prophets.

Matthew 7:12 KJV

The Lord Calls Upon Us to Be Cheerful in Spirit

...the cheerful heart has a continual feast.

Proverbs 15:15 NIV

A cheerful heart is good medicine,
but a crushed spirit dries up the bones.

Proverbs 17:22 NIV

Delight thyself also in the LORD; and he shall
give thee the desires of thine heart.

Psalm 37:4 KJV

Verily, verily, I say unto you, Whatsoever ye shall ask
the Father in my name, he will give it you.
Hitherto have ye asked nothing in my name: ask,
and ye shall receive, that your joy may be full.

John 16:23-24 KJV

Joy I will thank you, Lord with all my heart; I will
tell of all the marvelous things you have done.
will be filled with joy because of you. I will sing
praises to your name, O Most High.

Psalm 9:1-2 NLT

About Faith

Now faith is the substance of things hoped for,
    the evidence of things not seen.

Hebrews 11:1 KJV

For verily I say unto you, That whosoever shall say
  unto this mountain, Be thou removed, and be thou
cast into the sea; and shall not doubt in his heart, but
  shall believe that those things which he saith shall
    come to pass; he shall have whatsoever he saith.

Mark 6:23 KJV

Trust in the LORD with all thine heart; and
  lean not unto thine own understanding. In all thy
ways acknowledge him, and he shall direct thy paths.

Proverbs 3:5-6 KJV

I can do everything through him that
    gives me strength.

Phillippians 4:13 NIV

Cast your burden upon the Lord and He will sustain
you: He will never allow the righteous to be shaken.

Psalm 55:22 NASB

Our Faith Gives Us Courage

The Lord is my light and my salvation; whom shall
I fear? The Lord is the strength of my life;
of whom shall I be afraid?

Psalm 27:1 KJV

Yea, though I walk through the valley of
the shadow of death, I will fear no evil:
for thou art with me;
thy rod and thy staff they comfort me.

Psalm 23:4 KJV

But Jesus turned him about, and when he saw her,
he said, Daughter, be of good comfort;
thy faith hath made thee whole. And the woman
was made whole from that hour.

Matthew 9:22 KJV

...I tell you the truth, if you have faith as small as
a mustard seed, you can say to this mountain,
"Move from here to there" and it will move.
Nothing will be impossible for you.

Matthew 17:20 NIV

With God,
All Things Are Possible

And Jesus looking upon them saith,
  With men it is impossible, but not with God:
    for with God all things are possible.

Mark 10:27 KJV

Let every soul be subject unto the higher powers.
  For there is no power but of God:
    the powers that be are ordained of God.

Romans 13:1 KJV

Search for the Lord and for his strength,
    and keep on searching. Think of
    the wonderful works He has done,
    the miracles and the judgements
      He handed down.

Psalm 105: 4-5 NLT

…Be strong and courageous. Do not be terrified;
  do not be discouraged, for the Lord your God
      will be with you wherever you go.

Joshua 1: 9-10 NIV

About the Author

Jim Gallery lives and writes in Middle Tennessee. He serves as senior editor for both Brighton Books and Walnut Grove Press. In addition, Jim is a sought-after speaker and lecturer. He also has 20 year's experience as a pastor.

Jim is a graduate of the University of South Florida and the New Orleans Baptist Theological Seminary. He is the father of two children.

Some of his other titles include:

God Can Handle It
God Can Handle It... Teenagers
God Can Handle It... Fathers
Prayers of a Righteous Man
Prayers of a Dedicated Teacher